Ken & Chaos:
A Love Story

Ken & Chaos:
A Love Story

Katie Simpson

Copyright Page

Ken & Chaos: A Love Story
© 2025 Katherine Simpson

This is a work of nonfiction. Names, details, and identifying characteristics may have been changed to protect privacy. Any resemblance to actual persons, living or dead, is coincidental.

Published in the United States by Ember & Oak Consulting LLC, Montana. For inquiries please visit www.katiesimpsonbooks.com.

ISBN: 979-8-9931490-8-0
Cover design by Katie Simpson
Printed in the United States of America
First Edition

Dedication

For Ken.
My partner in chaos, my Dairy Queen date, my tractor-loving, turkey-dodging, tech-cursing, forever Valentine.
Life with you isn't always easy, but it's always worth it.

Acknowledgments

Writing this book reminded me just how many people it takes to survive chaos with laughter.

To Ken: thank you for being endlessly patient with me, for letting me tell our stories, and for laughing with me instead of at me (most of the time). You are the reason I have material and the reason I have love.

To my chosen family and friends: thank you for listening to the stories (probably more than once), encouraging me to keep writing, and reminding me that humor is meant to be shared.

To the readers: thank you for picking up this book. If you laugh, snort, or think, *"yep, that's my marriage too"* even once, then my job here is done.

And finally, to small towns, chickens, turkeys, tractors, Dairy Queen, and yes, even Siri, you gave me more material than I could ever have dreamed.

Preface

Every marriage has its own flavor. Some are polished and sophisticated, with anniversaries in Paris and picture-perfect Christmas cards. Ours? Not so much.

Ken & I built a life out of the everyday chaos of rural Montana. Our love story isn't filled with diamonds or yachts. It's filled with tractors, Dairy Queen dates, chickens with attitude, menopause mood swings, and one infamous grease fire. And through it all, through the disasters, the laughter, the eye rolls, and the turkeys, we've built something far more valuable than "perfect."

This isn't a fairy tale. It's not advice, or a marriage manual, or a self-help guide. It's just us. It's twenty-plus years of figuring out how to stay married when life keeps throwing curveballs. It's humor in the middle of frustration, love in the middle of chaos, and gratitude in the middle of all of it.

If you're looking for perfect, you won't find it here. But if you're looking for real, for messy, for laughter that keeps a marriage alive, welcome to our story.

Author's Note

This book was written before Ken's diagnosis. Before the doctors. Before the appointments and the long nights and the shifting ground beneath our feet.

I wasn't planning to publish it yet. Ken & Chaos was supposed to be a lighthearted project "for later," something fun we'd laugh about together when life slowed down a little. But life has a way of rewriting timelines, and suddenly "later" didn't feel like the right place anymore.

So I'm publishing it now.

For him.

Because these stories—the ridiculous ones, the tender ones, the grease-fire ones—are the truest reflection of who we are as a couple. They are the love we built long before cancer had a name. They are the chaos we survived together, the laughter that held us, and the everyday moments that made our marriage ours.

I didn't edit this book to match what we're walking through now. I didn't soften it, rewrite it, or insert wisdom I didn't have yet. I wanted it to stay exactly as it was the day I finished it—pure, funny, honest, and full of Ken in all his tractor-loving, kitten-adopting, turkey-dodging glory.

Because that's who he is.

And this is us.

Whatever the future holds (and we're taking it one day at a time) it has been my honor to be his wife. My privilege. My joy. The greatest chapter of my life.

If you laugh at these stories, I'm glad. If you see your own marriage in ours, even better. But if you walk away knowing what an extraordinary man Ken is—kind, patient, protective, stubborn, hilarious, and full of a steady love that carried me through more storms than I can count—then I've told this story right.

Thank you for reading our chaos.

Thank you for honoring him with me.

Thank you for holding a little piece of our love in your hands.

~Katie Simpson

Table of Contents

Copyright Page... 4

Dedication 5

Acknowledgments... 6

Preface... 7

Author's Note... 8

Chapter 1: Betty the Tractor............................... 12

Chapter 2: The Kitchen Massacre (A Ken Original Recipe) 14

Chapter 3: Vacations Gone Wrong..................... 17

Chapter 4: Home Improvement or Marital Endurance Test? 20

Chapter 5: Dollar Menu Dates and Dairy Queen Drive-Ins 22

Chapter 6: Love Is a Stocking............................. 25

Chapter 7: Ken the Protector (and Sometimes Model)..... 28

Chapter 8: The Secret: We Actually Like Each Other 31

Chapter 9: Chickens, Dogs, and Chaos (Otherwise Known as Tuesday).. 34

Chapter 10: Small Town Gossip and Tractor Envy.......... 37

Chapter 11: Camping, Fishing, and Other Forms of Torture 40

Chapter 12: The Romance of Rural Life (Mud Boots Included) 43

Chapter 13: The Sound of Silence (and Other Forms of Marital Miscommunication) 46

Chapter 14: Ken vs. Technology (Spoiler: Technology Wins) 51

Chapter 15: Kitten Fever (A Ken Epidemic) 54

Chapter 16: War Games and Marriage Counseling........... 57

Chapter 17: Middle-Age, Full Rage (and Still Married Anyways) 59

Chapter 18: Why Humor Is Our Love Language............. 62

Chapter 19: Happily Ever After 64

Bonus Chapter: The Man Cold 66

Closing Note 69

Chapter 1: Betty the Tractor

There are few things a man loves more than his woman. In Ken's case, it's his tractor.

One day he told me he was going to town to "price a wheelbarrow." You know, a simple, fairly inexpensive farm helper. Something practical. Something that doesn't require a financing plan.

Hours later, he came rolling back up the driveway with a sly grin and a brand-new blue tractor. A wheelbarrow? Please. He skipped right past Home Depot and went full-blown John Deere fantasy.

"Meet Betty!" he beamed, like a proud new father. "Isn't she wonderful?"

Betty, as it turns out, was shiny, loud, and apparently irresistible. Ken was practically drooling as he rubbed her fenders, patted her hood, and looked at me as if I should be equally smitten. He had this glazed-over expression usually reserved for teenage boys when they discover Sports Illustrated swimsuit editions.

I stood there in shock, trying to calculate how a wheelbarrow somehow multiplied itself into a tractor on the 20-mile drive to town. I mean, tractors don't exactly sneak up on you. There's no world in which you accidentally come home with a piece of heavy equipment.

But Ken? He was in love. From day one, Betty became his favorite "other woman." He talked about her horsepower, her hydraulics, her turning radius—all the things I never knew I'd need to pretend to care about. He waxed poetic about her like a man reciting Shakespeare.

And Betty? She has never spent a single night outside in the cold. Oh no, she lives in luxury. Parked neatly inside the shop, tucked away like royalty. Meanwhile, I'm the one scraping ice off my windshield in the dead of winter, but heaven forbid Betty's paint job gets frosty.

Ken even once suggested buying her a *sweater*—yes, a sweater—for those chilly Montana mornings. As if Betty might catch a cold. I had to remind him that she's a tractor, not a Pomeranian. But he was dead serious, muttering about how the weather "just isn't good for her" like she's some delicate Victorian lady who might faint at the sight of frost.

Me? I had questions. Big ones. Like: Did the tractor come with a seat for me, or should I just start walking to town now? How many chickens could I sell to cover this little surprise? And most importantly, could Betty cook dinner, or was that still my department?

Betty, for her part, didn't answer. She just sat there in all her gleaming glory, smug as hell. And from that day forward, I knew I had competition. Not with another woman, but with a tractor named Betty.

Chapter 2: The Kitchen Massacre (A Ken Original Recipe)

There are a few moments in marriage where you stop and think: *Is this love, or is this a fire hazard?* Valentine's Day with Ken landed firmly in both categories.

Ken had decided, in a sweet burst of romance, that he was going to cook me a Valentine's dinner. Not just any dinner, this was weeks in the making. He made secret grocery lists, whispered to cashiers like a man smuggling contraband, and guarded the pantry as if it held state secrets. For days leading up to it, he walked around with a smug grin, humming to himself like he had just cracked the Da Vinci Code of romance.

The big night finally arrived. I came home from work, tired, expecting maybe a card or some flowers, maybe takeout if I was lucky. Instead, I was greeted by the sight of smoke billowing out the open kitchen window like our house had taken up vaping.

I froze. Not because I thought the place was burning down—though it easily could have been—but because there was Ken, standing in the haze, flapping a towel around like a frantic air-traffic controller. His face was beet red, sweat dripping down his forehead, muttering the immortal words:

"Everything is fine. Don't worry."

For the record, when a man says *don't worry* while waving smoke out of the house, you should absolutely start worrying.

I stepped into the kitchen and was hit with the full crime scene. My curtains? Gone. They had been sacrificed to the grease gods, singed into oblivion. The walls? Spackled with some kind of oily abstract art, a Pollock painting done in bacon fat and despair. The stove looked like it had survived combat, and the floor was slick enough to qualify as a slip-and-slide.

And Ken? Ken acted like this was totally normal. He gave me this sheepish grin, as if torching my curtains and redecorating the walls in "Eau de Grease Fire" was just part of the ambiance.

"Dinner's ready," he said, with all the gusto of a man who had not just nearly burned down the house.

He ushered me to the table and proudly set down a plate. To my surprise, it didn't look terrible. A little...crispy, maybe. Slightly blackened. But not in an "insurance adjuster will call this an act of God" kind of way.

I tentatively took a bite. And you know what? It was delicious. Shockingly delicious. Like, "this man just committed arson but at least he can cook" delicious. We sat there together, eating quietly, as if nothing around us was covered in soot and grease.

Finally, I couldn't resist asking: "So… what happened?"

Ken shrugged, still chewing like this was a completely ordinary dinner. "Well," he said matter-of-factly, "I caught the pan of grease on fire. It…spread to the curtains. But don't worry. I'll fix it."

And then he added, with that same sheepish grin, "It was more important to me that you felt special tonight."

That's Ken. The man who will set fire to my kitchen in the name of love. The man who will nearly burn the house down but still serve me dinner with confidence. The man who reminds me, in his own chaotic, grease-splattered way, that romance doesn't always look like flowers and candlelight. Sometimes it looks like charred curtains, greasy walls, and the best damn Valentine's dinner I ever had.

Chapter 3: Vacations Gone Wrong

By now, you've probably figured out we are not sophisticated people. When we go on vacation, it's less *Eat, Pray, Love* and more *The Beverly Hillbillies Take a Field Trip*. Suitcases exploding, sunscreen applied like spackle, and enough snacks to survive the apocalypse. Subtle? Absolutely not.

Take the year we went to Hawaii. Paradise, right? Crystal water, palm trees, the whole travel brochure fantasy. Except when the Simpsons show up, it looks more like a sitcom gone wrong. First mistake? I overpacked. I didn't just bring outfits; I brought backup outfits for my outfits. By the time we landed, we looked like two pack mules stumbling through the Honolulu airport, sweating, red-faced, and already regretting our choices. Nothing screams "tourist" louder than dragging four oversized suitcases and looking like you've lost a fight with TSA.

But we pressed on. After all, this was Hawaii! Sunshine, beaches, mai tais. And then it happened. We got suckered into a timeshare pitch. You know the ones—they lure you in with free trinkets and promises of "just a short presentation." Next thing you know, you've been locked in a room for three hours while a man with too much hair gel explains "vacation equity" like it's the stock market.

Ken and I barely made it out alive, clutching our dignity like it was the last life raft on the Titanic. But we did manage to score the promised prize. A free dinner on a cruise ship.

Honestly, that dinner felt like we'd just beaten the system. We strutted out of that timeshare like two gladiators who had conquered the arena.

Naturally, we decided this victory called for shopping. Nothing says "celebrating your freedom" like blowing money at a tourist shop. We bought matching outfits, because nothing screams romance like polyester Hawaiian shirts and shorts that clash with everything in sight. Dressed in our tropical finest, we headed to the ship.

The second we boarded, they shoved alcohol into our hands. That should have been our first warning. You don't give unlimited booze to a couple like us unless you're prepared for chaos.

I, being the adventurous one, immediately wandered off to explore the ship. Top deck, ocean breeze, full panoramic views. I was living my best life. Meanwhile, Ken was back below deck, frantically searching for me like a husband in a Lifetime movie.

Finally, I spotted him, panicked, pacing, and looking like he'd lost his wife somewhere between the buffet and the life jackets. Without thinking, I leaned over the railing, cupped my hands around my mouth, and yelled,

"Ken! I'm up here and I'm not wearing any underwear!"

Heads turned. Drinks were spilled. A small child may have needed therapy. Ken, mortified, froze mid-step and looked up at me with an expression that said, *"Dear God, why do I love this woman?"*

Vacations don't make us look glamorous. They don't make us look cool, or sophisticated, or Instagram-ready. But they do make us laugh until our sides hurt, even if it's at our own expense. Especially at our own expense.

So no, we're not the couple sipping wine quietly on the balcony, gazing into each other's eyes. We're the couple who survived a timeshare ambush, dressed up like tropical clowns, and announced our underwear situation to half a cruise ship. And honestly? I wouldn't have it any other way.

Chapter 4: Home Improvement or Marital Endurance Test?

Ken and I have learned (and accepted) that we are not the best building partners. In fact, if there were a reality show called *Couples Construction Catastrophe,* we'd be the headliners.

It always starts the same way: one of us gets a bright idea. "Let's build a chicken coop!" "Let's add shelves in the shop!" "How hard can it be?" Those five words are the kiss of death for our marriage on project days.

Take the chicken coop. On paper, it looked simple enough. We had all the right pieces, we had the instructions, and we even had the optimism that comes right before disaster strikes. For the first fifteen minutes, we were practically Chip and Joanna Gaines, smiling, measuring, and pretending this was going to be a fun bonding activity.

Then the games began.

I handed Ken a piece of wood to cut. He told me which one. I confirmed. He nodded. Then he cut it and immediately realized it was the wrong piece. Suddenly, *I* was the problem. Apparently, I was supposed to read his mind and hand him the "right wrong piece" instead of the one he literally asked for.

I argued back, pointing out that I had followed instructions. Was it my fault he didn't double-check before revving up the saw like Tim the Toolman Taylor? Absolutely not. But logic has no place in construction arguments.

Within minutes, the whole project spiraled. Ken got mad and threw the tools down like he was declaring war. I got mad because he was being dramatic. Then I got *really* mad because I was hungry, and everyone knows you can't fight on an empty stomach. Next thing you know, Christmas was cancelled.

That's how it goes for us. What begins as "let's build something cute and functional" always devolves into yelling, eye-rolling, accusations, and at least one person storming off muttering about how the other person is impossible to work with. (Spoiler: we both say it.)

And yet, by some miracle, things eventually get built. The chicken coop stands. The shelves hold. The projects, despite the chaos, always get finished. They may not be perfectly square, and the instructions usually end up crumpled in the trash, but they get done.

I think that's the real lesson. Marriage isn't about building chicken coops in perfect harmony. It's about surviving the mess together. It's about realizing you can fight about wood measurements, threaten to cancel holidays, and still come back an hour later with a plate of food and an apology.

Because if we can survive building projects together? We can survive anything.

Chapter 5: Dollar Menu Dates and Dairy Queen Drive-Ins

In rural Montana, the concept of "date night" takes on a whole new meaning. Forget dinner and a movie. We don't even have a movie theater. No miniature golf, no comedy clubs, no late-night sushi spots. Unless you count watching cows chew cud under the stars, romance around here requires a bit of creativity.

Enter Ken's favorite date night magic: Dairy Queen.

That's right. While other couples are posting Instagram photos of candlelit bistros and rooftop cocktails, we're pulling into the Dairy Queen drive-thru, headlights illuminating the menu board like it's the Eiffel Tower. And let me tell you, in our world, the true symbol of romance isn't champagne—it's the *2 for $5 menu.*

Because nothing says "I love you" like two chicken strip baskets and a Blizzard. Inflation may have knocked out a few luxuries, but Dairy Queen still delivers.

Now, I'll admit it, Dairy Queen may not be the healthiest or fanciest date option out there. No waiter in a crisp white shirt is refilling my water glass, and the ambiance is less "fine dining" and more "sticky booth with a view of the ice cream machine." But Ken always makes it feel like a night out. He insists on it, actually. He makes sure that no matter how broke, tired, or overworked we are, we still carve out space to sit across from each other and eat french fries together.

That's what I've learned about love. It isn't about the money you spend. It isn't about grand gestures or exotic vacations (though if Ken ever wants to whisk me to Paris, I'll pack my bags faster than you can say "croissant"). It's about the effort. It's about showing up, even when the fanciest place in town is a Dairy Queen that closes at nine.

Ken has this way of turning ordinary into special. He'll slide the tray across the table with a grin, like he's serving me the chef's tasting menu at a five-star restaurant. He'll make corny jokes, tease me about stealing his fries, and insist on holding my hand across the sticky table. He makes me laugh, and that's the secret sauce you won't find on the menu.

And while the world might look at our version of date night and think, *Really? Dairy Queen?* I look at Ken and think, *Really. This is love.* Because when you strip it all down— when the curtains have been burned off your kitchen window, when the tractor has its own parking suite, when life feels more like chaos than order—what matters most is that someone still wants to sit across from you with a $2.50 burger and call it a date.

So no, we're not sophisticated. We're not fancy. We're not hashtag-worthy, picture-perfect, influencer-approved. But we're real. And real looks like two people who know that love isn't found in filet mignon or champagne toasts. Sometimes, it's right there in the Dairy Queen drive-in, with french fries between you and a Blizzard melting just a little too fast.

Chapter 6: Love Is a Stocking

Love takes many forms. Sometimes it's flowers. Sometimes it's chocolate. And sometimes it's your husband pulling one of your stockings out of his uniform shirt, in front of his entire workplace.

Ken used to wear uniforms to work, the kind of stiff button-up tops that look like they were designed by someone who thought fashion ended in 1974. Every morning he'd grab a clean one from the dryer, slap it on, and head out the door without a second thought.

One particular morning, he rushed out a little faster than usual. I heard the dryer door slam, heard him mutter something about being late, and then he was gone. No big deal. Or so I thought.

Mid-morning, my phone buzzed. It was Ken, texting me from work. *We need to talk,* the message read. Which, as any spouse knows, is never a good opener. I braced myself, half expecting he'd forgotten his lunch, lost his keys, or accidentally adopted another cat.

When he finally called, his voice was equal parts horror and disbelief.

"So," he began, "you're never going to believe what just happened."

Now, when Ken says that I always *do* believe it. Because with Ken, the unbelievable is practically routine.

Apparently, halfway through his morning, he'd started to feel something rubbing against his back under his uniform shirt. At first, he ignored it—probably chalked it up to the shirt being stiff or maybe a scratchy tag. But as the day went on, the rubbing got more noticeable. Finally, he ducked into the bathroom, tugged off the shirt, and discovered the culprit.

One of my stockings.

Wedged into the back of his shirt like some kind of bizarre lingerie hitchhiker.

And of course, because it's Ken, this discovery did not happen in private. Oh no. He pulled that stocking out in front of a group of coworkers, holding it up like Exhibit A in the trial of "Why I Should Check the Dryer More Carefully."

The room, he said, went silent. Then the laughter started.

"Nice, Simpson," one guy apparently called out. "Dressing up for us today?" Another chimed in, "Well, at least you've got good taste!"

Ken wanted to sink into the linoleum. Instead, he stuffed the stocking into his pocket, buttoned up his shirt, and marched back out with whatever dignity a man can have after stripping lingerie out of his work clothes at nine a.m.

When he told me the story later, I couldn't stop laughing. Tears-down-my-face, can't-breathe, stomach-cramp laughing. Ken, meanwhile, wasn't nearly as amused. "You could've just left me a *note*," he grumbled. "Something simple. Like, 'Love you, have a good day.' That would've sufficed. Not...this."

That *was* love. Not intentional, not scripted, not Instagram-worthy. Just one of those ridiculous little accidents that turns into a story you tell for years. Because love isn't always about candlelit dinners or romantic speeches. Sometimes it's about laughing so hard you nearly choke because your husband smuggled your pantyhose into a staff meeting.

And honestly? I think I prefer it that way.

Chapter 7: Ken the Protector (and Sometimes Model)

Ken is my sometimes protector. In all things.

Now, when I say protector, you might think of the traditional stuff: locking the doors at night, chasing off sketchy salesmen, answering the door in his underwear and a gun belt. And yes, Ken does all of that. But sometimes, his role as protector stretches into territory I never expected.

Take the day I was trying to hem a dress.

Now, I am not a seamstress. I am barely qualified to sew on a button without making it look like a toddler's craft project. But there I was, dress in hand, nearly in tears because I couldn't figure out how to measure the hemline correctly. I tugged, I pinned, I sighed dramatically, muttering things like, "Why can't I just buy clothes that fit?" The whole scene was one needle short of a meltdown.

Enter Ken.

He walked into the room, took one look at me, and without a word grabbed the tape measure. With all the seriousness of a man defusing a bomb, he bent down, measured carefully, and made a few marks. Then, as if it were the most logical thing in the world, he grabbed my dress and left the room.

Before I could even process what was happening, Ken reappeared in my dress, and declared, "Here. This is where the hem should go."

I froze. My husband was standing in my dress. Modeling. Like this was some kind of farmyard fashion show.

Yes. The *dress.*

I can still see it in my mind, Ken, all six feet of him, walking out in my dress like he was auditioning for a very niche runway show. He twirled. He posed. He showed me exactly where the hemline needed to be.

I was horrified. I was also laughing so hard I couldn't breathe. Tears were streaming down my face, my hands shook too much to hold the pins straight, and I'm pretty sure that hemline ended up looking like it had been drawn by someone riding a rollercoaster.

Ken, meanwhile, was completely unfazed. To him, this wasn't about pride or dignity. It was about helping me get through a problem, protecting me not from danger this time, but from myself. From my frustration, my meltdown, my spiral into dress-related despair.

That's Ken. He doesn't just protect me from the big scary stuff in life. He protects me from the small, silly moments that could easily ruin a day. He steps in, puts on the pants— or the dress, apparently—and does whatever it takes to lighten the load.

And maybe the hem was crooked. Maybe the dress never looked quite right after that. But in that moment, what mattered wasn't the hemline. It was the man in the dress, reminding me that laughter is the best kind of protection there is.

Chapter 8: The Secret: We Actually Like Each Other

People sometimes look at Ken and me and ask, "What's your secret?" We've been together for over twenty years, and apparently, in today's world, that makes us something of a curiosity. Like we should be in a museum exhibit titled *Long-Term Relationships: Rare and Endangered Species.*

Our relationship isn't perfect. Not even close. We argue. We bicker. We disagree about stupid things like how to fold towels or whether Betty the Tractor deserves her own sweater. We've had our share of slammed doors and icy silences. We've weathered serious storms—money worries, health scares, family drama, the kind of challenges that could easily break a couple apart.

And yet, here we are. Still standing. Still laughing. Still choosing each other, even on the days when one of us would rather choose a nap and some personal space.

So what's our secret? It's simple. We actually like each other.

That might sound obvious, but you'd be amazed how many couples skip this part. They love each other, sure. They're committed. They're bound by mortgages, kids, or the sheer inertia of time. But do they *like* each other? Do they genuinely enjoy one another's company, not just tolerate it?

That's where Ken and I found our magic. We like hanging out. We like sitting in the Dairy Queen parking lot with fries between us. We like binge-watching terrible TV shows and yelling at the screen together. We like laughing at our own ridiculousness, like the time he modeled my dress or the time I shouted about underwear from the deck of a cruise ship.

We like each other in the big ways and the small ones. Ken is the person I want to tell my news to first—whether it's good, bad, or downright stupid. He's the one I want in the passenger seat when life goes sideways. And sometimes, when I catch him across the room, doing nothing particularly special—just tinkering with a project, or eating ice cream, or smiling to himself—I think, *Yep. That's my person. Still him. Always him.*

Do we drive each other crazy? Absolutely. I'm not trying to sell you some Hallmark-card version of marriage where everything is soft-focus and candlelight. Real love is messy. It's surviving home improvement projects without filing for divorce. It's arguing over who left the milk out and then laughing about it an hour later. It's being mad, then hungry, then mad because you're hungry.

But underneath it all, there's a bedrock of genuine friendship. And friendship, that quiet, steady liking of each other, is what has carried us through twenty years and counting.

So when people ask us for the secret, I smile. I could talk about communication, compromise, or patience. I could pretend there's some elaborate recipe for success. But the truth is much simpler.

We like actually each other.

And honestly? That's enough.

Chapter 9: Chickens, Dogs, and Chaos (Otherwise Known as Tuesday)

If there's one word that sums up our life, it's *chaotic*. Not glamorous chaos. Not "fun weekend getaway" chaos. More like "why is there livestock in my driveway and mud in my coffee" chaos.

At some point, I decided that our little farm needed variety. Chickens were fine, sure, but I wanted something different, something to spice up the flock. So, I brought home turkeys. Little, fluffy, adorable turkey poults who peeped sweetly and looked like they'd grow up to be gentle, majestic birds strutting across the yard.

Oh, how naïve I was.

Those turkeys grew up to be hitmen.

Not just your average backyard birds, either. No, these boys appointed themselves my personal security detail. Forget the dogs, they were useless compared to the turkeys. The minute I stepped outside, my feathered entourage would fall in line. Left, right, center—flanking me like trained bodyguards. And heaven help anyone who tried to come within six feet of me.

The UPS driver? Escorted back to his truck. Friends who dared to visit? Surrounded and herded off the property like criminals. Even Ken wasn't immune. The turkeys would eye him suspiciously, as if to say, "We know you're married to her, but we're watching you."

It would have been flattering if it wasn't also terrifying.

Imagine walking outside every day with three puffed-up, red-faced turkeys shadowing your every move, gobbling ominously at anyone who dared to approach. I couldn't garden, couldn't hang laundry, couldn't even check the mailbox without my turkey SWAT team by my side. I was never alone. Ever.

And it wasn't just their protective instincts that were out of control. No, these boys had hobbies. Destructive hobbies. They destroyed what little yard we had left, pecking and scratching until our grass looked like it had been hit by a tornado. And worse, they taught the chickens new tricks. As if the chickens weren't already chaotic enough, now they had turkey mentors leading them down a darker path. It was like watching a gang initiation play out in my own backyard.

Ken, of course, thought this was hilarious. He'd sit on the porch, sipping his coffee, chuckling as I tried to outrun my self-appointed bodyguards. I'd glare at him while dragging a rake through the wreckage of what used to be my flower beds, the turkeys gobbling in solidarity beside me.

As much as I complained, as much as I groaned about the yard and the chickens learning "new skills," there was something oddly comforting about it all. Those ridiculous turkeys loved me. Fiercely. Overprotectively. They saw me as their person, and in their own chaotic way, they made sure I was safe.

Our life may not be orderly, and our yard may never make the cover of *Better Homes & Gardens,* but it's never dull. It's loud, messy, unpredictable, and sometimes just plain ridiculous. But when I step outside and feel that rush of chaos—dogs barking, chickens plotting, turkeys marching into formation—I can't help but laugh.

Because chaos may not be pretty. But it's ours.

Chapter 10: Small Town Gossip and Tractor Envy

Living in a small town is…interesting. On one hand, it's peaceful. You know your neighbors, people wave when they drive by, and there's always someone willing to lend you a tool or a cup of sugar. On the other hand, *everybody* knows *everything,* or at least they think they do. Gossip is basically the town's favorite sport.

Ken has embraced this fully. He is the self-appointed neighborhood hall monitor, sitting on the porch or peering out the window, watching every suspicious vehicle that drives down our dirt road. If a truck slows down even a little, Ken is on it. "Never seen that one before," he'll mutter, narrowing his eyes like Clint Eastwood in a spaghetti western. He knows who belongs, who doesn't, and exactly which neighbor ordered a new lawnmower based on delivery truck frequency.

He considers it his duty to make sure no one steals the neighbors' stuff. I think he likes to imagine himself as the unofficial sheriff, armed with nothing more than a coffee cup and righteous indignation.

Me? Not so much. I tend to stay inside and work. I don't know every vehicle, every face, every rumor floating around. My idea of community surveillance is listening to the dogs bark and assuming they've got it handled.

And that's how we ended up with one of my favorite small-town stories. For months, everyone thought Ken had an imaginary wife.

See, Ken was always out there waving to people, talking to neighbors, fixing things, protecting the road. He was visible. Present. Reliable. The kind of guy who becomes a familiar fixture, like the stop sign at the corner or the old tractor rusting in a field.

Me, on the other hand? I was almost never outside. Between working, writing, and avoiding poultry death squads, I didn't spend much time mingling. So, from the neighbors' perspective, Ken lived alone.

They'd see him out mowing, chatting, watching the road. They'd wave, he'd wave back, and that was that. Weeks passed. Months. Still no sighting of "the wife."

Apparently, the rumor mill kicked into overdrive. Did Ken have a wife, or was she just a convenient cover story? Had he made me up to sound respectable? Was I locked in the attic like some Montana version of *Jane Eyre*?

Finally, one day, I did venture outside (probably escorted by turkeys, knowing my luck) and the looks I got were priceless. Neighbors blinked in shock, like they'd just spotted Bigfoot.

"You're real!" one of them actually said.

Real. As if Ken had been parading around town with tales of a mythical spouse that no one believed. For months, I'd apparently been downgraded from wife to urban legend.

To this day, I still tease him about it. "How's your imaginary wife doing?" I'll ask, sipping my coffee while he glares good-naturedly. The neighbors, at least, are satisfied now that I make occasional appearances to prove I exist.

That's small-town life, though. Nothing is private, everything is exaggerated, and your absence from a few potlucks is enough to spark a conspiracy theory. But honestly? I kind of love it. Because beneath all the gossip and tractor envy, there's comfort in knowing people notice you, even if they think you're imaginary.

Chapter 11: Camping, Fishing, and Other Forms of Torture

One thing about living in Montana is that there's no shortage of outdoor activities. Camping, fishing, hiking, hunting, it's basically the state's entire personality. People move here for the wide-open spaces, the fresh mountain air, the rivers teeming with trout. It's paradise… if you're into that sort of thing.

Ken? Loves it.

Me? Hard pass.

I don't camp. Period. Ever. The thought of crawling into a flimsy nylon tent, zipping it closed, and calling it "home" for the night makes my skin crawl. It's not peaceful; it's terrifying. I don't want to wake up next to a spider the size of a Buick or listen to mysterious rustling outside the tent flap at two in the morning while Ken whispers, "It's probably nothing." That "nothing" has teeth in Montana. No, thank you.

And don't even get me started on the bathroom situation. You want me to *pee outside*? Absolutely not. Squatting in the woods like a terrified raccoon while praying no one stumbles by? Hard no. I like my plumbing indoors, preferably porcelain, and ideally within twenty feet of a coffee pot.

Fishing isn't much better. Ken can stand on a riverbank for hours, casting and waiting, patient as a monk. I cannot. I can't even be quiet long enough to pretend I'm fishing. The idea of standing still, whispering, and holding my breath while staring at water makes me twitchy. Within five minutes I'm humming, tapping my foot, or blurting out something like, "So… do the fish know we're here?" which, according to Ken, "scares them off." Honestly, if fish are that sensitive, maybe they deserve to be scared.

But Ken loves it. He loves the crisp air, the rhythm of casting, the quiet. And because he loves it, sometimes I try. I've gone along on a few trips, attempted to fake enthusiasm, even pretended that sleeping on an air mattress in a damp tent was "adventurous." Usually, by morning, I'm cranky, sore, and bargaining with God to make it stop raining so I can go home.

We don't have to love all the same things. Ken finds peace in the woods; I find mine in my writing or curled up with a good book. He'd happily live in a cabin with no electricity, and I'd happily live in a world where "glamping" meant a cabin with Wi-Fi and indoor plumbing.

And somehow, it works.

Because the truth is, even though I don't camp and I don't fish, I love that Ken does. I love the way his eyes light up when he talks about the river, the quiet pride in his voice when he describes the perfect cast. I love that he finds joy in things I don't understand, because it reminds me that marriage isn't about becoming clones of each other, it's about appreciating the differences.

So no, you won't catch me peeing in the woods anytime soon. You won't find me sleeping in a tent or standing silently on a riverbank with a fishing pole. But you *will* find me cheering Ken on from the sidelines, hot shower waiting at home, ready to listen to his fish stories (even if I suspect they're exaggerated).

Because love doesn't mean always joining in. Sometimes, it just means being glad your person has something they love—even if you're never, ever going camping.

Chapter 12: The Romance of Rural Life (Mud Boots Included)

People love to romanticize rural life. They picture sunsets over rolling fields, fresh eggs collected in a cute little basket, and couples holding hands while strolling through wildflowers. It's all very Hallmark-channel-meets-Instagram.

The reality? Chicken shoes.

If you don't know what chicken shoes are, consider yourself blessed. Around here, they are a necessity. They're the dedicated shoes that never, under any circumstances, leave the chicken pen. You don't wear them to the store. You don't wear them in the house. You don't even wear them to take out the trash. Chicken shoes are for chickens, period.

Because chickens are messy. And by messy, I mean disgusting.

The bottoms of our chicken shoes are basically encased in four inches of what I'll politely call "goop." A layered cake of mud, manure, straw, and whatever else happens to fall in a chicken run. The kind of substance that adds two inches of height to your shoe and makes you feel like you're wearing platform boots—if platform boots also smelled like death and despair.

Cleaning them is a ritual. You grab the hose, blast away as much of the gunk as possible, and watch it slough off in sheets, like some kind of horror movie special effect. No matter how much you spray, though, there's always a little left behind. Chicken shoes never fully recover. They carry the scars forever.

It's not glamorous. In fact, it's the opposite of glamorous. There's nothing sexy about watching your spouse wrestle with a hose, trying to clean off boots that look like they've survived a natural disaster. There's nothing romantic about the smell that wafts through the yard on a hot summer day when the shoes are "drying."

And yet... this is our life.

The romance of rural life isn't in the picture-perfect moments people imagine. It's in the messy practical details. It's in knowing which pair of shoes is safe to wear inside and which ones belong permanently by the back door. It's in laughing when one of us forgets and accidentally tracks "chicken goop" onto the porch. It's in the shared understanding that yes, this is gross, but it's also part of the life we chose together.

Ken and I may not stroll hand in hand through fields of wildflowers very often, but we do stand side by side in the chicken yard, wearing our ridiculous chicken shoes, managing the chaos together. And honestly? That feels more romantic to me than any Hallmark fantasy ever could.

Because at the end of the day, love isn't about flowers or sunsets. It's about chicken shoes and the person who doesn't mind wearing them with you.

Chapter 13: The Sound of Silence (and Other Forms of Marital Miscommunication)

There are days when Ken and I communicate like a well-oiled machine. We finish each other's sentences, anticipate what the other needs, and have full conversations with nothing more than raised eyebrows and muttered sarcasm.

And then there are the other days.

The days when we seem to speak completely different languages. When I'm saying one thing, he's hearing another, and somehow we both end up mad without knowing exactly why. It's like emotional charades except no one wins and there's definitely no trophy.

The truth is, when you live and work together 24/7, you'd think communication would be our superpower. Unfortunately, it's not. We have entire conversations that make zero sense. One of us starts mid-thought, the other responds to something entirely different, and before you know it, we're both standing in the kitchen arguing about whether "I said maybe" actually means "no."

But nothing exposes our communication flaws quite like *The Phone Situation.*

We both have cell phones. You'd think that would make life easier. After all, we live on a small property. I'm in the house; he's usually in the shop or backyard, maybe 100 feet away. How hard could it be to get ahold of each other?

Very. Apparently, very.

Because Ken forgets to turn his ringer on. Every. Single. Day.

Without fail, I'll be trying to call him because I need help, or have news, or maybe just found a chicken wearing something it shouldn't. I'll call once. Nothing. Twice. Still nothing. By the fifth call, I'm pacing like a hostage negotiator, muttering, "Answer the phone, Ken. Just answer the damn phone." By the tenth, I'm ready to fake my own disappearance just so he'll notice I exist.

Finally, I give up and stomp outside, phone in hand, half composing a eulogy for my sanity. I'll circle the house, call again, listen for a ringtone, and hear absolutely nothing. Then, there he is. Sitting in the backyard, perfectly relaxed, completely oblivious, smiling at the chickens like Snow White on a coffee break.

"Did you not hear your phone?" I'll snap.

"Oh," he says casually, "I forgot to turn the ringer on."

He says it like he forgot to pick up milk. Like it's a small thing. Meanwhile, I've gone through all five stages of grief and a minor cardiac event.

"You couldn't hear it?" I ask, incredulous.

"I didn't know you were calling," he says, completely unfazed.

Once (this deserves a book plate of its own), I had to drive to the city for a work thing. It's an all-day trip, and I don't do the solo-commute tango well (it's a horrible drive, long, and there are zero bathrooms that resemble civilization). I called Ken to see if he would come with me. No answer. Fifteen text messages, no answer. Eight phone calls, no answer. I walked every inch of the property like I was playing Where's Waldo. I peeked inside the shop, looked behind the tractor, even looked in the chicken coop because by then I was desperate.

His truck was in the driveway. All the farm equipment was in their usual awkward positions. Nothing. I finally threw my hands up, hopped in my car, and left without him. Feeling furious, flustered, and feeling betrayed by my own homestead.

An hour later he calls.

"Hey," he says, casual as a man ordering coffee. "I took a nap in the shop."

A nap. In the shop. An hour ago. When I'd texted him that this trip mattered, that I needed him to come. I could have throttled him. Instead, I did what any rational partner would do. I seethed in the driver's seat, rehashing every argument we ever had, scowled out the window, and silently planned a revenge that involved him missing Dairy Queen for a week.

Our miscommunications are sometimes small and silly. Sometimes it blows up into something I'd like to strangle. But mostly, it becomes a story we tell at family dinners. Me, red-faced and dramatic; him, sheepish and probably still napping somewhere.

That's when my eye starts twitching.

Because by that point, it's not about the phone anymore. It's about everything. Every forgotten text, every missed message, every moment I've been talking to thin air while he's out there serenading livestock. I've been left emotionally on *read* by a man who doesn't know his ringer's off.

And of course, he has the nerve to act surprised that I'm mad. "What's wrong?" he'll ask, as if the ten missed calls and smoke coming out of my ears are somehow mysterious.

Then comes the silence. The long, dramatic, passive-aggressive silence that could win an Oscar. We'll pass each other in the kitchen like rival mob bosses, no one making eye contact, both waiting to see who breaks first.

Ken's tactic is simple: food.

When he knows he's in trouble, he provides food. It's his love language and his truce offering rolled into one.

I'll hear him rummaging around in the kitchen, banging pots just loud enough for me to notice. Then comes the smell—bacon, because who can stay mad when bacon is involved—and I can feel my resolve weakening. Ten minutes later, a plate slides quietly in front of me.

No words. No "I'm sorry." Just a peace offering in the form of food.

And damn it, it works.

Because he knows me. He knows that no matter how irritated I am, I can't stay mad when there's food involved. My anger may be righteous, but my stomach is weak. By the time I've taken the first bite, he's already back in my good graces.

He'll look over and grin. "Better?"

I'll sigh, shake my head, completely forgetting why I was mad in the first place and say, "This is delicious."

That's us. We don't always communicate perfectly. We misfire. We misread. We miss calls, literally and figuratively. But somehow, we always find our way back to each other, usually through humor, occasionally through snacks.

It's okay to get upset. It's okay to be frustrated with each other. That's part of being human and being married. What matters is that, at the end of the day, you find your way back to each other.

Marriage isn't about perfect communication. It's about learning how to laugh when you can't. It's about knowing that sometimes silence speaks volumes, and sometimes the best apology doesn't come with words; it comes with fries.

Chapter 14: Ken vs. Technology (Spoiler: Technology Wins)

Ken is many things: strong, resourceful, protective, hilarious. But when it comes to technology? He's a walking disaster.

It's not just that he's "bad with phones." No, that would be too simple. Ken's relationship with technology is like watching a man wrestle an alligator. It's dramatic, loud, and destined to end with him flat on his back while the alligator waddles away victorious.

Take his phone, for example. It is not uncommon for Ken to accidentally block people. Friends, family, coworkers, they'll text him, and suddenly they're gone. "Weird," he'll mutter, frowning at the screen like it's personally betrayed him. "Guess they just don't text me anymore." No, darling. You blocked them. Again.

One time, he somehow managed to change his entire phone to Spanish and couldn't figure out how to change it back. For two days, he wandered around muttering things like "¿Qué significa *configuración*?" and "Why does my phone keep calling me *amigo*?" I offered to fix it, but he was determined to "figure it out himself." He tried but only made it worse. Eventually, I took pity on him and switched it back before he accidentally enrolled us in an online bullfighting class.

And then there's Siri. Poor Siri.

Ken has a habit of yelling at her, convinced she's deliberately misunderstanding him. "CALL MIKE!" he'll bark, and Siri will calmly reply, "Calling Mom." "No! MIKE!" he yells, and Siri, bless her heart, replies, "Would you like to call Michael's Pizza?" By this point, Ken is red-faced, sputtering, "I DON'T WANT PIZZA, SURI!"—because yes, he calls her *Suri,* like she's Tom Cruise's daughter.

What really gets him, though, is when Siri talks back. He'll freak out like he's in a sci-fi movie and the machines have finally risen. "She ANSWERED me!" he'll whisper, horrified. "She's listening all the time!" Yes, darling. That's literally her job.

But the pièce de résistance—the crown jewel of Ken's tech disasters—was the infamous group chat incident.

One night, feeling particularly romantic, Ken decided to text me a list of all the sweet, mushy things he had in mind. Dinner ideas. Weekend plans. Maybe even a little "rated PG-13" suggestion or two. It was heartfelt, thoughtful, and… accidentally sent to every single one of his friends in a group chat.

Imagine his horror when his phone lit up with replies: "Uh, thanks, buddy, but I'm not into long walks on the beach with you." "I appreciate the offer, but I'll pass on the bubble bath." The poor man nearly threw his phone into the river.

Ken, mortified, tried to play it off. "Just testing the group chat!" he stammered, which, of course, only made it worse. His friends still bring it up years later. "Hey, Ken, you planning another romantic evening for us?" they'll tease, and he turns the color of a ripe tomato.

As much as I laugh at his technological mishaps, I secretly love them. They remind me that behind all the chaos, Ken's intentions are always good. He blocks people by accident, but he'd never shut anyone out on purpose. He yells at Siri, but only because he wants things to work. And that group chat disaster? It was embarrassing, sure, but it was also proof of how much he cares. His friends just got a front-row seat to it.

So yes, technology always wins in our house. But if loving me enough to risk texting the entire neighborhood is wrong, I don't really want Ken to win.

Chapter 15: Kitten Fever (A Ken Epidemic)

Some men buy sports cars when they hit midlife.

Ken adopts kittens.

And not just any kittens. Tiny, homeless, squeaky, hopelessly adorable balls of fluff that could melt the heart of a tax auditor.

It always begins the same way, a harmless scroll through kitten videos that quickly spirals into trouble. A slow, creeping sickness I've come to call *Kitten Fever*.

The first symptom is subtle. Ken's social media feed mysteriously fills with kitten videos. Every scroll is meows, purrs, tiny paws kneading blankets. I'll hear him chuckling softly, phone in hand, and that's when I know.

The fever has started.

"Look," he'll say, tilting his phone toward me with a grin.
"Aren't they *soooo* cute?"
And just like that, I'm on high alert.
I start watching him like he's on a watch list.

The next stage hits fast: the reconnaissance phase. That's when he starts casually mentioning that the shelter "appears" to have a lot of kittens for adoption. Appears. As if the universe just *accidentally* texted him that information.

"I was just looking," he'll say. Sure, and I was just window-shopping when I came home with a tractor named Betty.

I remind him, gently but firmly, that we are full. Our house already sounds like a petting zoo after dark. We do not need another furry mouth to feed or another reason for me to step on a toy mouse at 3 a.m.

He nods, pretending to agree, but then the next symptom hits: the justification phase.

"Maybe we should just stop by the shelter and make a donation," he'll suggest innocently.

"We already did," I remind him.

"Well," he counters, "maybe they need *more* donations." Ken suddenly becomes the Mother Teresa of stray cats.

That's when I know we're in trouble.

Because once Ken "goes to town to run errands," anything is possible. He might come back with tractor parts, or lumber, or (God help me) a baby feline wearing a bowtie.

And then it happens.

I'll hear the truck pull up, the door creak open, and there he is, standing in the doorway with a ridiculous grin and a cardboard box.

Inside is one itty-bitty, wide-eyed kitten. Gazing at Ken with such love and adoration.

"Look," he says softly, holding it up like he's presenting Simba to the animal kingdom, "isn't he so cute? He needs me."

Oh, Ken. He does not need you. You need *him*.

And just like that, the house is rearranged again. Food bowls multiplied, another litter box appears, and I'm back to trying to remember which kitten belongs to which of Ken's "errands."

I can never stay mad for long. Because when I see Ken stretched out on the couch with that tiny ball of fluff asleep on his chest, his hand gently scratching its head, I melt a little too.

That's Ken. Big, tough, tractor-wielding, turkey-dodging Ken, softened by eight ounces of purring fur.

So yes, I roll my eyes, and yes, I swear we're done adopting *this time*.

But deep down, I know the cycle will repeat again.

Because in our house, kitten fever is chronic, contagious, and absolutely incurable.

Chapter 16: War Games and Marriage Counseling

There are a few lessons every couple must learn the hard way.

Ours? If we want to stay married, we can never, ever, under any circumstances, play video games together.

It started innocently enough. Ken suggested we "bond" over a co-op shooter.

"How hard can it be?" I asked, blissfully unaware I was about to single-handedly destroy our marriage and an entire digital village.

Within minutes, Ken was barking military jargon like he'd been redeployed.

"Protect my six!" he yelled.

"My what?" I shouted back, mashing buttons like I was typing an angry email. My character spun in circles, then crab-walked sideways into a wall and falls over.

Ken was dodging bullets, diving behind crates, taking out enemies with surgical precision, while I looked like a toddler trying to ice-skate for the first time.

"Shoot! Shoot!" he screamed.
"I am shooting!" I yelled, as my character tossed a grenade at our own team.

Smoke everywhere. Ken's digital soldier flew through the air like an action-movie extra, landing dramatically in front of me.

Game over. Marriage pending.

He turned to me in real life, disbelief on his face.
"You were supposed to cover me!"
"I was covering you!" I protested. "I was spinning!"
"That's not cover, Katie, that's some weird dance."

The post-battle debrief lasted longer than the game itself. Ken launched into a full lecture on tactical positioning, flanking maneuvers, and something about "combat awareness." Halfway through, I started crying, not because I cared about the mission, but because my character still couldn't stand up straight.

We agreed to retire from virtual combat that night and for the sake of national security and our marriage.

Now, whenever Ken suggests a "fun couples activity," I make sure it involves zero controllers, no respawn button, and absolutely no friendly fire.

Because love may conquer all but it does not survive Call of Duty.

Chapter 17: Middle-Age, Full Rage (and Still Married Anyways)

Menopause. Just the word is enough to make most women sigh and most men run for cover. It's like puberty's evil twin—except instead of giving you acne and a bad attitude, it gives you hot flashes, mood swings, and a strong desire to throat-punch anyone who chews too loudly.

Poor Ken.

The man has been through it all; kitchen curtains going up in smoke, vacations gone wrong, and turkeys acting like mob enforcers. But nothing prepared him for me in the throes of menopause.

It started with the hot flashes. One minute I'd be fine, the next I'd be ripping off layers of clothing like I was auditioning for a Vegas revue show. Ken would come into the room, look at me fanning myself with a magazine, and cautiously ask, "Everything okay?"

"NO, KEN, IT'S NOT OKAY," I'd snap, drenched in sweat, glaring at the thermostat like it had personally betrayed me. "WHY IS IT 95 DEGREES IN HERE?"

He'd quietly point out that it was, in fact, 68 degrees. Which, of course, only made me angrier. "DON'T ARGUE WITH ME. I'M MELTING."

Then came the mood swings. One second I'd be weepy over a commercial about paper towels, the next I'd be furious because Ken left a spoon in the sink. "Do you even CARE about me?" I'd demand, waving the spoon like Exhibit A in a courtroom. Ken, bless him, would look confused but still manage to keep a straight face.

He's learned a few survival tactics along the way. He always has a fan nearby, ready to plug in at a moment's notice. He keeps snacks stocked because apparently menopause is fueled by rage and carbohydrates. And most importantly, he's figured out when to talk and when to slowly back out of the room without making sudden movements.

What I love most, though, is that he doesn't make fun of me. Oh, sure, he'll crack a gentle joke now and then, like calling my hot flashes "my personal power surges." But he never makes me feel crazy, even when I *am* acting a little crazy. He just... shows up. He sits with me through the mood swings, hands me water when I feel like I'm combusting, and reminds me (softly, from a safe distance) that this, too, shall pass.

Marriage isn't just about the fun stuff—the Dairy Queen dates, the vacations gone wrong, or the chaos of chickens. It's also about surviving the unglamorous seasons. The times when your body feels like it's staging a coup, your emotions are unpredictable, and you're not exactly your best self.

Ken may not fully understand menopause (honestly, I don't either), but he understands me. And that's what matters.

So yes, middle age comes with full rage. Yes, I've snapped at him for breathing too loudly and threatened to burn the house down if he touches the thermostat again. But he's still here. Still laughing with me, still loving me, still willing to weather the storm—even when the storm is hormonal and sweats through the sheets at 2 a.m.

And that, my friends, is how you know you've got the right person.

Chapter 18: Why Humor Is Our Love Language

Every relationship has its ups and downs. People grow, people change, people argue. Even the strongest marriages have moments where it feels like everything is about to self-destruct. And ours is no different.

The difference is how we handle it.

For us, the secret has always been humor. Humor is our love language.

When the chickens are out terrorizing the yard, the tractor is stuck in the mud, and I'm threatening to move to town just to get a break, Ken doesn't fight fire with fire. He cracks a joke. When I'm mid-menopause meltdown, fanning myself like a lunatic and cursing the thermostat, he smirks and calls it my "personal power surge." And when he manages to text an entire group of friends about his romantic plans for me, I laugh so hard I can't breathe.

We meet in the middle, and we meet in laughter. Always.

It doesn't mean we don't argue. Oh, we do. We've bickered over wood measurements, vacation disasters, and what constitutes "real food" at Dairy Queen. But even in the middle of our most ridiculous fights, one of us eventually cracks. Someone makes a face, someone says something sarcastic, and the tension breaks. We end up laughing, and just like that, the world feels lighter again.

Laughter doesn't erase the problem, but it makes it survivable. It softens the edges. It reminds us that the person across from us isn't the enemy, they're the teammate we chose. The one we're in this with, no matter how messy it gets.

But humor isn't the only glue. Respect is, too.

Ken and I made a rule early on. No matter what, we always treat each other with respect. That means saying "please" and "thank you." It sounds small, but it's huge. Those little words remind us not to take each other for granted. They remind us that love is built in the details—in the way you hand someone a cup of coffee, in the way you acknowledge the effort it took to feed chickens in the snow, in the way you don't dismiss each other's frustrations, no matter how silly they sound.

We've learned that the world will throw enough challenges our way. Life is messy. Work is stressful. Families are complicated. The least we can do is make home the place where laughter lives, where kindness matters, and where even when we're irritated, there's still gratitude in the room.

So no, we don't have a perfect marriage. But we have one built on humor and respect, and that's what has carried us through twenty years and counting.

Because at the end of the day, Ken makes me laugh, and I make him laugh. And if you can still laugh together, really laugh, then everything else is negotiable.

Chapter 19: Happily Ever After

People love the phrase "happily ever after." It's how every fairy tale ends, tied up neatly with a bow, as if love erases hardship and everything after "I do" is sunsets and roses.

Truthfully, happily ever after is a myth. It's an unrealistic expectation. Real life doesn't work that way. There are bills, laundry, sick days, arguments, burned kitchen curtains, menopause, and the occasional turkey mafia patrolling the yard. No one is happy *all the time.*

What I've learned is that the real magic isn't in some mythical "ever after." It's in choosing the right partner, for the right reasons, and showing up for each other no matter what. That's where the love grows. Not just in the easy seasons, but especially in the hard ones.

Life is hard. There's no instruction manual. We're all just fumbling our way through, doing the best we can with the tools we've got. But having a foundation of love and laughter—having a partner who makes you laugh when you want to cry, who listens when you rant, who steadies you when you stumble—that's a blessing. One I will never take for granted.

Ken is that blessing for me.

He is patient when I am not. He is kind when I'm in full rage mode. He is human, imperfect, sometimes clueless, and often hilarious. He is the voice of reason when my world feels overwhelming. He is the one who, against all odds, makes chaos feel like home.

So no, we don't have a fairy-tale happily ever after. What we have is better. We have a real, messy, beautiful life together. We have laughter. We have respect. We have twenty years of proving that liking each other is just as important as loving each other.

And if you ask me, that's as close to happily ever after as anyone can get.

Bonus Chapter: The Man Cold

Ken is tough. He can wrangle a stubborn tractor, chase off sketchy vehicles on our dirt road, and even survive a full-blown grease fire in the kitchen without flinching. But give the man a cold? Suddenly, we're one sneeze away from calling the undertaker.

I swear, the man cold is its own medical condition. It's not the flu, it's not pneumonia, it's not even a bad case of allergies, it's worse. According to Ken, it is the absolute end of days.

It always starts the same way. He'll sniffle once, look vaguely tragic, and announce in a gravelly voice, "I don't feel so good." Within minutes, he's wrapped in a blanket like a Victorian orphan, stretched out on the couch, sighing dramatically. The remote control will be three inches from his hand, but suddenly, it's too far. "Babe," he croaks, "can you… can you change the channel? I can't reach it."

I roll my eyes, but of course I hand him the remote. Because nothing's more dangerous than a man left alone with daytime television when he's convinced he's on his deathbed.

Within an hour, he's convinced he's running a fever. "I'm burning up," he groans, one hand on his forehead, the other clutching a tissue box like it's a lifeline. I pull out the thermometer. 98.9 degrees. "See?" he gasps. "I told you. I'm practically boiling." For context, that's barely warmer than a latte.

Meals become a whole production. "I don't think I can eat solids," he'll whisper, as if chewing a sandwich is an Olympic event. "Maybe just soup. But not too hot. Or too cold. And maybe with some crackers. But not the salty ones." By the time I'm done playing nurse-slash-short-order-cook, I'm the one who deserves the medal.

And don't even get me started on the noises. The groaning, the coughing, the dramatic sighs—he sounds like an extra in a war movie, bravely clinging to life while whispering his final words. If I had a dollar for every time Ken muttered, "I think this is it, babe," we could fund a vacation somewhere warm enough to sweat the germs out.

Now, here's the strange part. The man cold never lasts more than 48 hours. Two days of absolute drama, and then, like magic, Ken bounces back, bright-eyed and bushy-tailed, ready to conquer the world again. Meanwhile, I'm left with the actual cold I caught from him—because, of course, I *will* catch it—and do I get to collapse dramatically on the couch for two days? Nope. I still feed chickens, wrangle turkeys, and cook dinner while sneezing my face off.

But you know what? As much as I complain, as much as I tease him mercilessly when he's back on his feet, there's something endearing about it all. Because under all the toughness, under the tractors and the porch-sheriff routine, Ken's just human. Vulnerable. A little pitiful, even. And maybe, just maybe, it's nice to be reminded that he needs me, even if it's just to hand him the remote.

So yes, Ken can handle grease fires, poultry gangs, and Montana winters. But when the man cold strikes? All bets are off.

Closing Note

Marriage isn't about being perfect. It's about finding the person who will laugh with you when the tractor gets stuck, bring you Dairy Queen on a Tuesday night, and let turkeys chase them off the porch because they're too devoted to you to argue.

If this book made you laugh, reminded you of your own chaos, or gave you a little hope that love can survive grease fires, menopause, and the man cold, then I've done my job.

Here's to finding joy in the mess, laughter in the arguments, and love in the middle of it all. Because sometimes, chaos isn't what you survive. It's what stitches you together.

~Katie